S0-ASU-651

FAMILIES

BOOK 2

Senior Author
Dahia Shabaka

**Published by
Metropolitan Teaching
and Learning Company**

Reginald Powe
President

Juwanda G. Ford
Managing Editor

The Office of Social Studies, under the auspices of the Division of Educational Services, selected a cadre of educators to create early elementary social studies instructional materials. All of the individuals listed in the categories below were or are teachers or administrators with the Detroit Public Schools.

Senior Author: Dahia Shabaka

Authors: Marva Brown, Barbara Calloway, Janet Fulton, Marie Harris, Annie Mae Holt, Cathy Johnson, Chaka Nantambu, Cynthia A. Spencer, Dr. Patsy Stewart, Charles W. Sumner

Project Editor: Dr. Jonella Mongo

Acknowledgments: David Adamany, Chief Executive Officer, Detroit Public Schools; Juanita Clay Chambers, Associate Superintendent, Division of Educational Services, Detroit Public Schools; Ellen Stephens, former Deputy Superintendent, Division of Educational Services, Detroit Public Schools; Kwame Kenyatta, Committee on Educational Quality

METROPOLITAN PUBLISHING STAFF

Managing Editor: Juwanda G. Ford

Production: Cheryl Hudson

Design Staff: Virginia Graziano, Martha Grossman, Charles Yuen

Editorial Staff: Linda Ekblad, Elspeth Leacock, Bruce T. Paddock, Jennifer Rose

Copy Chief: Joyce M. Gaskin

Photo Research: Romy Charlesworth, Rory Maxwell

Copyright ©2000 Metropolitan Teaching and Learning Company. Published by Metropolitan Teaching and Learning Company. All rights reserved. No part of this book may be reproduced or utilized in any form or by any means, electronic or mechanical, including photocopying, recording, or by any information storage and retrieval system without permission in writing from the publisher.

For information regarding permission, write to the address below.

Metropolitan Teaching and Learning Company
33 Irving Place
New York, NY 10003

Printed in the United States of America
ISBN: 1-58120-821-9

CONTENTS

UNIT 4 Family Needs and Wants

UNIT **5** Families Around the World

UNIT 6 Families and Technology

Reference Section

Ford Model T's sold for $500 in 1908.

FAMILY NEEDS AND WANTS

There are some things that all people need to live. There are other things that people want. In a family, people work together to get things they need and want.

FAMILIES HAVE NEEDS AND WANTS

Like everyone, Khari has needs. **Needs** are things people must have in order to live. Food is a need. Khari eats a big breakfast before going to school. He needs good food like juice and cereal to help him grow.

Khari needs warm clothing to protect him from cold weather. Clothing is a need.

Khari's home keeps him safe from cold, snow, or rain. Any place that keeps people safe from the weather is called **shelter**. Shelter is a need. Love is also a need. All of Khari's family members share love.

Khari's family gives him the things he needs. However, he wants other things, too. **Wants** are things people would like to have, but do not need in order to live. Khari wants a new bike.

Sometimes wants are things that you do.
Khari wants to go to the water park. He
does not need to go to the water park.
He likes to go because it is fun.

1. What are some of your needs?
2. What are some of your wants?

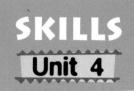
Seasons

During the year the weather changes. These changes are called seasons. In Detroit, the seasons are spring, summer, fall, and winter. Jasmine has a garden in Detroit. Look at how the garden changes each season.

SPRING

Day by day the weather gets warmer. New leaves grow on the trees.

SUMMER

The weather is hot. Jasmine wears shorts and a tank top to keep cool.

Answer these questions about seasons in Detroit.

1. During which season could you make a snowman?

2. What clothes would you wear during the different seasons?

3. During which season would you plant seeds?

FALL

The weather becomes cooler. Leaves change color and fall from the trees.

WINTER

The weather is cold. Sometimes it snows. Jasmine wears a hat, a coat, and mittens to keep warm.

FAMILIES USE GOODS AND SERVICES

At night, Pam sleeps under a warm blanket. In the morning, her alarm clock rings. She puts on a dress and a pair of shoes. Pam's parents bought the blanket, alarm clock, dress, and shoes for her. Things that people buy and sell are called goods.

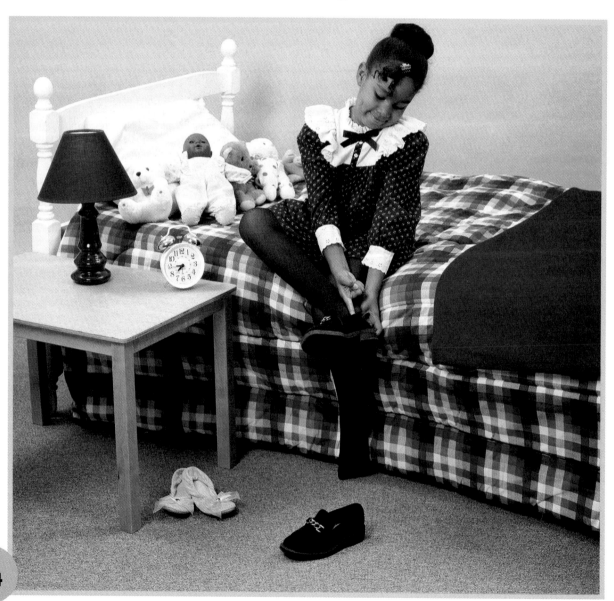

All day, Pam uses goods her family has bought. For breakfast, Pam has cereal, toast, and orange juice. After breakfast, Pam brushes her teeth. The cereal, bread, orange juice, toothbrush, and toothpaste are all goods.

Families buy goods. They also pay for services. A **service** is work that helps other people.

A postal worker helps Adam's grandpa send a package. The dentist keeps Jamal's teeth healthy. A librarian reads a story to Michelle, Malika, and Ivy.

A teacher helps students learn to read and write. The postal worker, the dentist, the librarian, and the teacher all provide services.

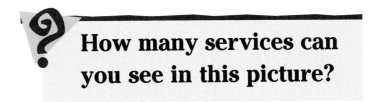

How many services can you see in this picture?

3 WORKING FOR WHAT WE NEED AND WANT

Catrina's family works to get the things they need and want. Catrina's mother works in a lab. She works with other scientists to find new cures for diseases. Catrina's father repairs telephone lines.

Catrina's mother and father bring home money from their jobs. Last year, they used the money they made to buy their own house.

Catrina's family works inside their home, too. Grandmother cares for Catrina and her sister. That is work, even though she doesn't get paid. Grandmother provides a service for the family. Grandfather builds toys. People pay him for the toys he makes.

Catrina helps her family with the things they need. She cleans her room. She folds her clothes. She sets the table for dinner. She gives her family her love.

How do families get the things they need and want?

Using Picture Graphs

This picture shows quarters, dimes, and nickels. Count the quarters. Count the dimes and the nickels. How many of each are there?

You can use a picture graph to show how many of each coin you counted. A picture graph uses pictures to show how many. How many of each coin does the chart show?

How Many Coins Do I Have?	
Quarters	🪙 🪙 🪙 🪙
Dimes	🪙 🪙
Nickels	🪙 🪙 🪙

Our class made a picture graph. Each of us said what we want to be when we grow up. Some of us want to be doctors. Some of us want to be firefighters. Use the picture graph to answer the questions.

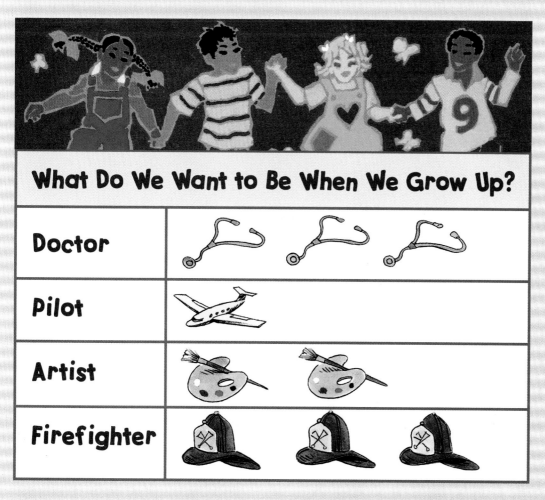

What Do We Want to Be When We Grow Up?

Doctor	
Pilot	
Artist	
Firefighter	

1   How many students want to be doctors?

2   How many students want to be artists?

3   What job does only one student want?

BRINGING GOODS TO THE FAMILY

Your family buys goods. Bread and cereal are goods made from wheat. Wheat grows from seeds farmers plant in the ground.

Farmers pick the ripe wheat with a special machine. Then trucks take the wheat away.

Most of the wheat goes to a mill. At the mill, wheat is made into flour.

Some of the flour is sent to factories where it is made into goods like bread and cereal. These goods are sent to stores.

At the local market, your family buys the goods made from wheat. You buy bread, cereal, noodles, crackers, and flour. Your family pays for these goods and takes them home.

1. **What else grows on farms?**

2. **What happens to wheat between the farm and your home?**

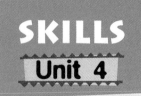

Details

The main idea of a piece of writing is the most important idea. A **detail** tells you more about the main idea.

Read "A Trip to the Grocery Store." The main idea is that the writer bought a lot of things at the store. Can you name details that tell about the main idea?

A Trip to the Grocery Store

We bought lots of things at the grocery store. We bought broccoli and lettuce. We bought bread and cereal. We bought soap. We bought pie plates.

We bought broccoli and lettuce is one detail. What other details did you find?

Now read the advertisement below.

Sam's Supermarket

Sam's Supermarket has new services for you. A cook will show you how to bake a cake. The store also has a baby-sitter to care for your children while you shop. Now Sam's also has helpers to carry your bags to the car.

1 What is the main idea of the advertisement?

2 What are the details that tell about the main idea?

REVIEW
Unit 4

Word Wrap

Use these words to complete the sentences.

service　　　　**goods**　　　　**want**

shelter　　　　**need**

1 A new doll is a _____ .

2 Fighting fires is a _____ job.

3 An apple and a bicycle are both
_____ .

4 A family needs _____ like a house or apartment.

5 A warm coat for the winter is a _____.

Unit Wrap

All people need food, clothing, shelter, and love. People might want things, too. Some people work outside the home. Some people work in the home. They buy goods and services with the money they earn. Everyone in a family can give their love.

?

1. **What is the difference between needs and wants?**

2. **What is the difference between goods and services?**

Using Picture Graphs

Imani and her father went to the grocery store. The picture graph shows how many of each item they bought. Use the picture graph to answer the questions.

What Did We Buy at the Store?	
Milk	🥛 🥛 🥛
Bread	🍞 🍞
Apples	🍎 🍎 🍎 🍎
Cheese	🧀
Corn	🌽 🌽 🌽 🌽

1 How many apples did Imani and her father buy?

2 What did they buy the least of?

3 How many ears of corn did they buy?

FAMILIES AROUND THE WORLD

People around the world meet their needs in different ways. They eat different kinds of food. They wear different kinds of clothing. They live in different kinds of homes. They speak different languages, too. And they celebrate different days and events.

LIVING IN MALI

My name is Babatu. *Babatu* means "peace maker." I live in Mali. Mali is a hot, dry country in Africa. A **country** is a land in which the people share a group of laws.

There are many kinds of homes in Mali. Some families live in houses made of clay. Other families live in dome-shaped houses lined with beautiful mats.

In Mali, many families have their own farms. They eat most of the food they grow. They sell the extra food at the market. Some people make goods, like bread, to sell.

Some of us wear traditional African clothes. A woman may wear a head wrap called a *gele*. A man may wear a loose shirt called a *dashiki*.

There are many festivals in Mali. Mali is also famous for its puppet shows. We love to celebrate with our families and neighbors.

What is special about where you live?

LIVING IN THE DOMINICAN REPUBLIC

My name is Rafaela. My family lives in the Dominican Republic. It is always hot here.

This is our home. The walls are made of wood. The roof is made of tin.

The Dominican Republic is on an island. After school, I like to go to the beach. My three brothers like to practice with their band. When I see them in a parade, I shout, "¡Hola!" *Hola* is "hello" in Spanish.

We have a special kind of music
in my country. It is called *merengue*.
Every year we have a merengue festival.
Music fills the air and people dance in
the streets.

We celebrate many events in our communities. We also celebrate with our families. We had a big party on my sister's birthday. We ate avocado salad, yellow rice, pork, seafood salad, yuca, sausage, and fried plantains. We call these plantains *tostones*.

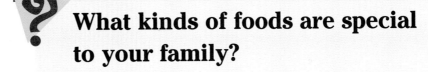

What kinds of foods are special to your family?

3 LIVING IN CANADA

"*Bonjour!*" That means "hello" in French. My name is Juliette. I live in Quebec. Quebec is a big city in Canada. Where I live there are four seasons. Spring, summer, and fall are short and cool. Winter is very long and cold.

I live with my family in a brick apartment house. We heat our apartment to keep it nice and warm. The brick keeps the heat in and keeps the cold out.

My friends know a lot of ways to have fun in cold weather. Every year there is an ice carnival. People build beautiful ice sculptures. We dress in warm clothing to play in the snow.

My family celebrates special days like
birthdays and anniversaries. We have
parties and give gifts. One day we had a
special cake for my grandparents'
anniversary.

1. **What is the weather like
where you live?**

2. **How do you have fun with
your family?**

Using Globes and World Maps

The planet we live on is called Earth. Earth is shaped like a ball. It has seven large areas of land. These large areas of land are called continents. Earth also has four large bodies of water. These large bodies of water are called oceans.

NORTH POLE

SOUTH POLE

You can see the continents and oceans on a globe. A globe is a small model of Earth. Like Earth, a globe has a **North Pole** and a **South Pole**. The North Pole is near the top of the globe. The South Pole is near the bottom.

This is how Earth looks on a flat map.
You can see all the continents and the
four oceans.

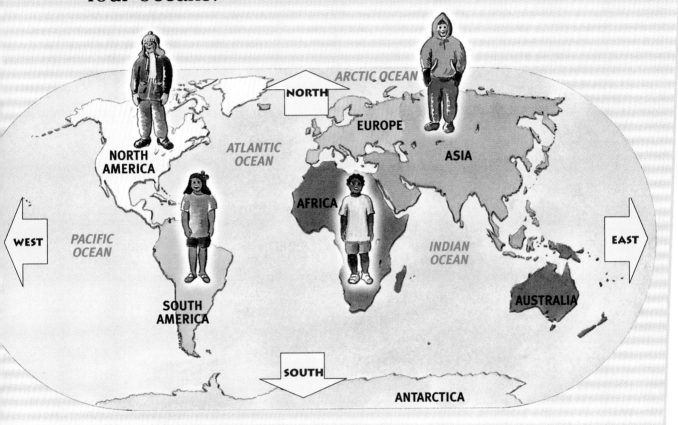

1 Look at the people in the far north.
Are they dressed for a cold or a hot climate?

2 Look at the people in the middle part of
the map. Are they dressed for a cold or
hot climate?

LIVING IN VIETNAM

My name is Minh. I live in southern Vietnam. It rains a lot here. The rainy season lasts nine months, from March until November. The dry season is only three months long. It lasts from December through February.

My family uses a boat to go to the market. The market is in boats, too.

My family's house is on the Mekong River. Our house keeps us dry during the rainy season.

During the rainy season, I wear a raincoat to school. My raincoat is big. It fits over my bicycle. Almost everyone I know rides a bicycle to get around.

Each year, families celebrate Tet. *Tet* is the Vietnamese New Year. It doesn't last just one day. It lasts for months. There are parties and fairs. We exchange gifts. We eat special cakes made from rice.

What do you wear when it rains?

121

LIVING IN JORDAN

My name is Ali. I live in a country called Jordan. It is very dry in my country.
My family lives in a house made of stone. The stone keeps the inside of my house cool when it is hot out.

Part of Jordan is a desert. Sometimes it does not rain in the desert for more than a year.

Many women in Jordan wear long dresses. Their clothes protect them from the weather, wind, and sand.

Some of our everyday foods are pita bread, hummus, lamb, and eggplant. We have special meals, too. We observe Ramadan for one month. At the end of Ramadan there is a delicious feast.

Families and friends celebrate special events, such as marriages. We all say *"tahanina"* to the bride and groom. It means "congratulations."

How does your home keep you warm in the winter and cool in the summer?

ALL AROUND AFRICA

Africa is a huge continent with over 50 countries. It has cold places, hot places, dry places, and wet places. The top of Mount Kilimanjaro is cold and covered with snow. The Sahara is dry. The grasslands are hot.

African families live in many different kinds of homes. Some Africans live in beautiful houses made of clay. Others live in houses on stilts. Many Africans live in big apartment buildings.

127

African people
speak many
different languages.
They wear different
kinds of clothes.
They eat different
kinds of foods.

African families celebrate many things. They celebrate when a baby is born. They celebrate weddings. These students in Nigeria are celebrating their graduation at the end of the school year.

What does your family celebrate?

Word Wrap

Use these words to complete the sentences.

continent   country   globe   ocean

1 People in a _____ share a group of laws.

2 South America is a _____.

3 An _____ is a large body of water.

4 A small model of Earth is called a _____.

Unit Wrap

All families are proud of who they are, where they live, and what they do. We celebrate who we are. We also learn how others are both like us and different from us.

? What are some ways that people around the world are alike and different?

Using Globes and World Maps

This world map shows all the continents.
It shows the oceans, too. Read aloud the
names of each continent and ocean.
Then answer the questions.

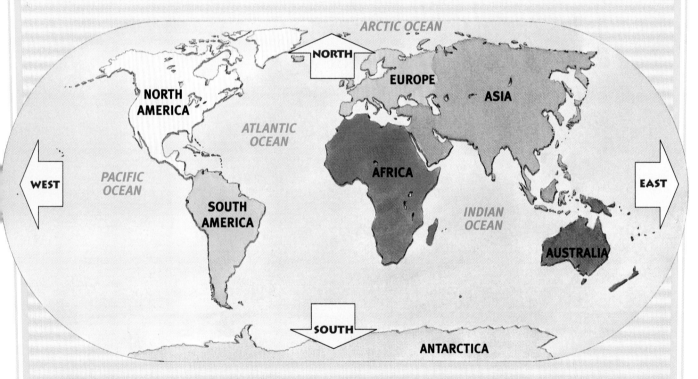

1 How many continents are there?

2 How many oceans are there?

3 Which continent is north of South America?

4 Which ocean is south of Asia?

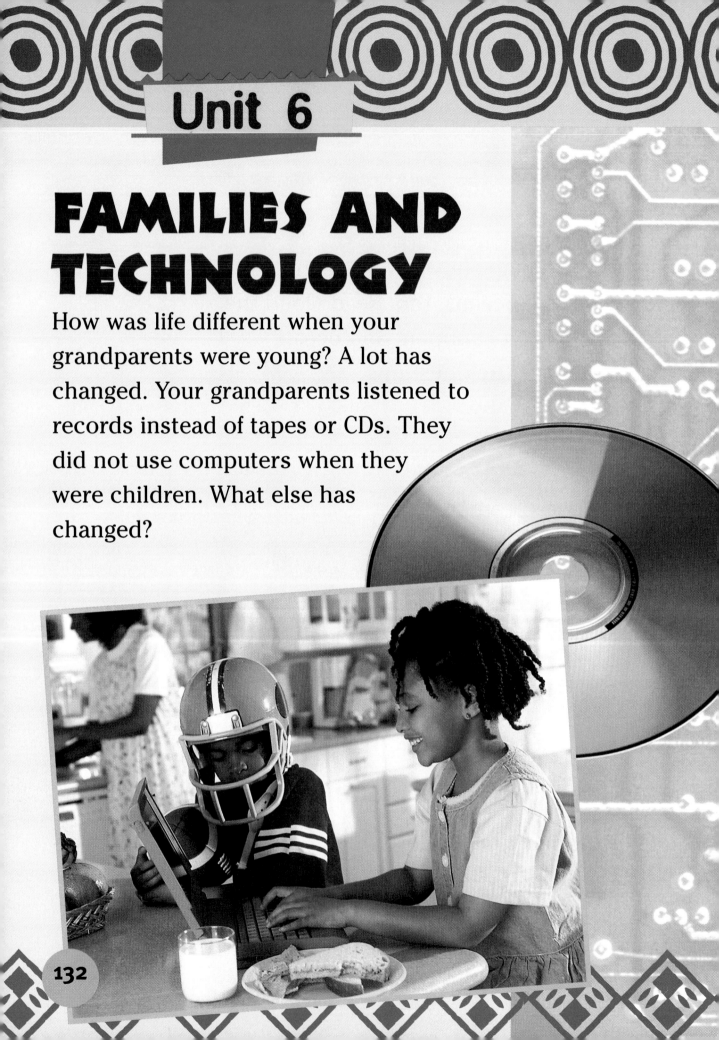

Unit 6

FAMILIES AND TECHNOLOGY

How was life different when your grandparents were young? A lot has changed. Your grandparents listened to records instead of tapes or CDs. They did not use computers when they were children. What else has changed?

USING THE COMPUTER

Karen's family has a computer in their home in Detroit. Karen uses E-mail to write letters to her cousin Jason. Jason also has a computer. He lives in California. He can read Karen's letter right after she sends it.

File Edit Go Bookmarks   3:00 PM
E-Mail
Location: http://www.home/karen

To:Jason
From:Karen

Dear Jason,
Do you know how cars
looked a long time ago?
I have to find out for school.
I hope you come to visit soon.
Love,
Karen

Karen also uses the computer to draw pictures. She likes to play computer games, too. She uses the computer to do her schoolwork. Today, she needs to find out about old cars.

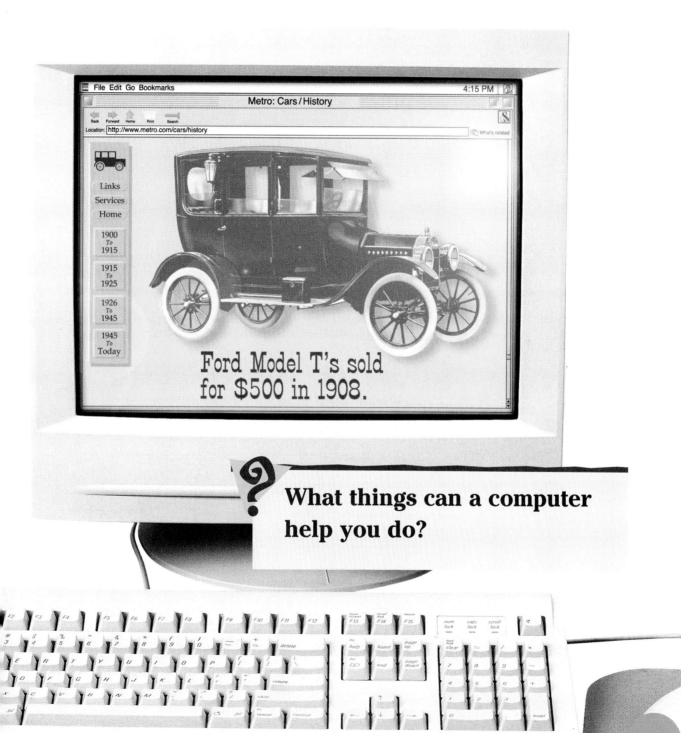

File Edit Go Bookmarks   4:15 PM

Metro: Cars / History

Back   Forward   Home   Print   Search

Location: http://www.metro.com/cars/history   What's related

Links
Services
Home

1900
To
1915

1915
To
1925

1926
To
1945

1945
To
Today

Ford Model T's sold
for $500 in 1908.

What things can a computer help you do?

Using Bar Graphs

Karen wanted to show how many hours she used the computer. She made a graph titled "Hours on the Computer." A **bar graph** uses bars to show how many. Karen filled in one square for each hour. Count the blue squares above Sunday. How many hours did Karen use the computer on Sunday?

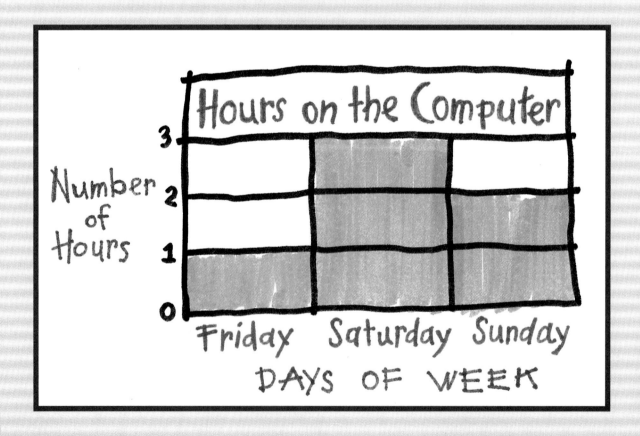

Jason made a bar graph, too. It shows how many toys he packed in his backpack. It shows how many of each kind he packed. Each square stands for one toy. Read the title of the bar graph. Read the words at the bottom of the bar graph. Then answer the questions.

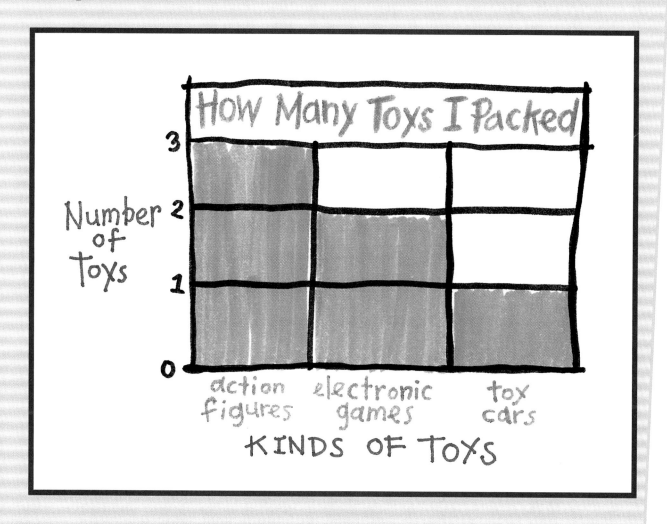

1   What kinds of toys did Jason pack?

2   How many toy cars did he pack?

3   How many action figures did he pack?

STAYING IN TOUCH

Families today use technology to stay in touch.
They use different kinds of telephones.
Cordless phones work all over the home and even
outside. Cell phones can go in a pocket or a bag.
Cell phones work almost anywhere you go.

138

Some families use pagers to reach each other. Some families use computers or fax machines. Today, it is easier to stay in touch with the people we love.

How do you stay in touch with the people in your family?

HAVING FUN

Andy and Eric have toys with remote controls. When they press a button, the toys move. Different buttons can make the toys turn right or left or go slow or fast.

Some families make their own videos. Then they can watch the videos on their VCRs. Other families play video games. Families use technology to have fun.

What are some ways that you use technology to have fun?

LOOKING BACK

Long ago, people used coal or wood to cook their food. Can you find the oven in this picture? Look at the lamp above the sink. It looks different from lamps today. It used oil.

Today, people use gas or electricity to cook their food. Can you find the modern oven? Look at the lights above the sink. They use electricity. What else do you see that uses electricity?

Thirty-five years ago, most families did not own color televisions. TV pictures were in black and white. There were no CD players then. There were no VCRs. There were no video games.

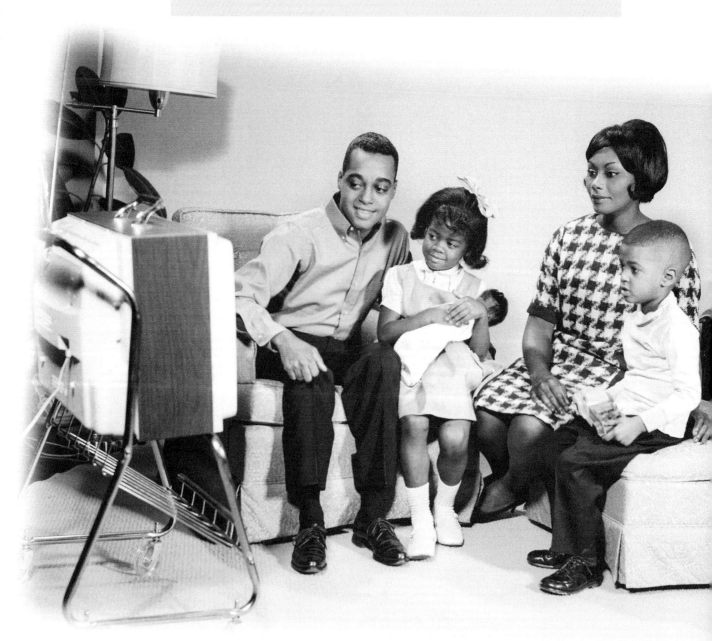

This is an electronics store today. This store sells televisions. It also sells CD players and VCRs. CD players and VCRs are recent inventions. Televisions are not new but they have been improved a lot.

Long ago, many people worked together to build one car. One person put the wheels on the car. Another person painted the car. Inspectors checked the cars for safety.

Today, car factories look very different. There are fewer people. Machines called robots do many jobs. Computers test cars to make sure they are safe.

1. How has technology made life easier for some families?

2. Do you think technology has made life hard for some families?

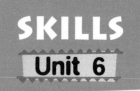

Making Predictions

A **prediction** is a guess about what will happen. To make a good prediction, you use what you already know.

Look at the picture. Then make predictions as you answer the questions.

1 Who will win the race?

2 What else can you guess by looking at the picture?

Make predictions about what will happen next. Look at the picture and use what you already know. Then answer the questions.

1 What will the man do next?

2 What will the dog do next?

3 Tell the reasons for your predictions.

Word Wrap

Use these words to complete the sentences.

prediction   **bar graph**

1 A _____ shows how many.

2 A _____ is a guess about what will happen next.

Unit Wrap

Life is always changing. New inventions help you learn, talk to people, and play. They help you get work done. Your grandparents didn't have computers, VCRs, or remote controls when they were young. As you grow older, technology will change.

? **How is your home different from your grandparents' home?**

Using Bar Graphs

The Carver family has radios, telephones, and computers. The bar graph shows how many of each they have. Use the bar graph to answer the questions.

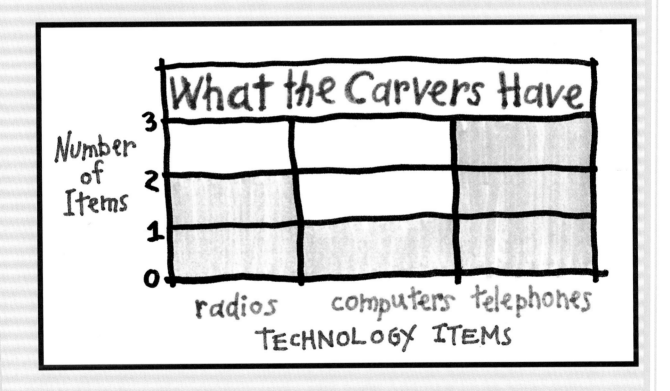

1 What kind of item do the Carvers have the most of?

2 What kind of item do they have the fewest of?

3 How many radios do they have?

151

ARCTIC OCEAN

RUSSIA

ALASKA

CANADA

PACIFIC OCEAN

NORTH

WASHINGTON

MONTANA

OREGON

IDAHO

WYOMING

PACIFIC
OCEAN

NEVADA

UTAH

COLORADO

WEST

CALIFORNIA

ARIZONA

NEW MEXICO

HAWAII

PACIFIC
OCEAN

MEXICO

SOUTH

CANADA

RTH DAKOTA

MINNESOTA

Lake Superior

MAINE

VERMONT

NEW HAMPSHIRE

TH DAKOTA

WISCONSIN

Lake Huron

Lake Michigan

MICHIGAN

Lake Ontario

NEW YORK

MASSACHUSETTS

RHODE ISLAND

CONNECTICUT

Lake Erie

NEBRASKA

IOWA

INDIANA

OHIO

PENNSYLVANIA

NEW JERSEY

ILLINOIS

DELAWARE

Washington, D. C.

MARYLAND

KANSAS

MISSOURI

WEST VIRGINIA

VIRGINIA

EAST

KENTUCKY

OKLAHOMA

ARKANSAS

TENNESSEE

NORTH CAROLINA

SOUTH CAROLINA

MISSISSIPPI

GEORGIA

ALABAMA

ATLANTIC

TEXAS

LOUISIANA

OCEAN

FLORIDA

★ National capital

THE WORLD

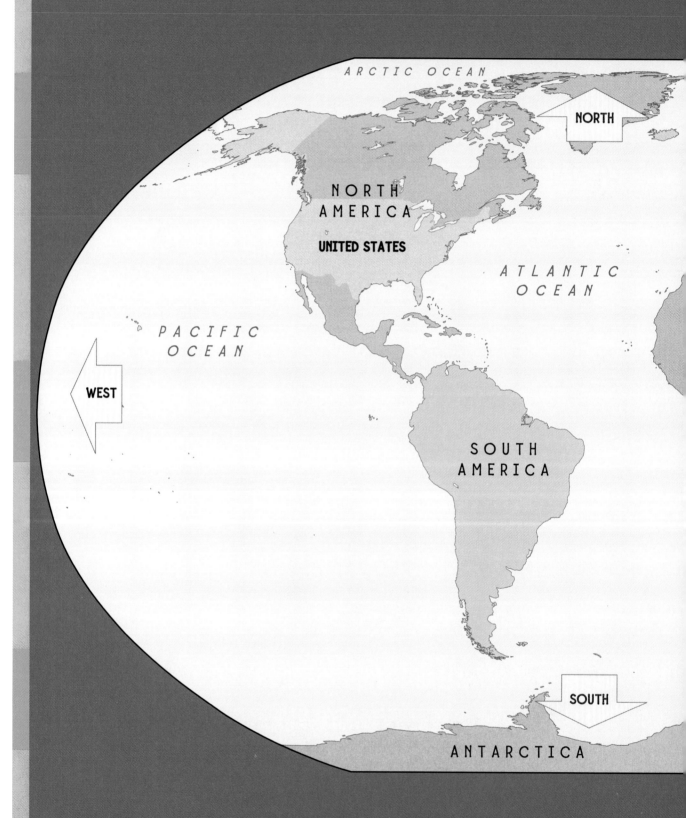

ARCTIC OCEAN

NORTH

NORTH
AMERICA

UNITED STATES

ATLANTIC
OCEAN

PACIFIC
OCEAN

WEST

SOUTH
AMERICA

SOUTH

ANTARCTICA

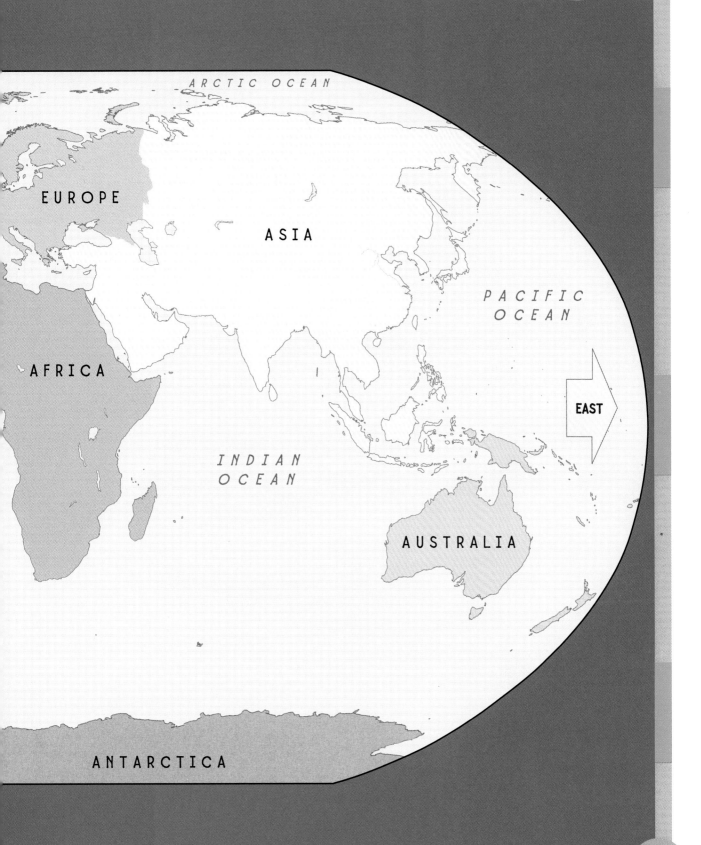

ARCTIC OCEAN

EUROPE

ASIA

PACIFIC
OCEAN

AFRICA

EAST

INDIAN
OCEAN

AUSTRALIA

ANTARCTICA

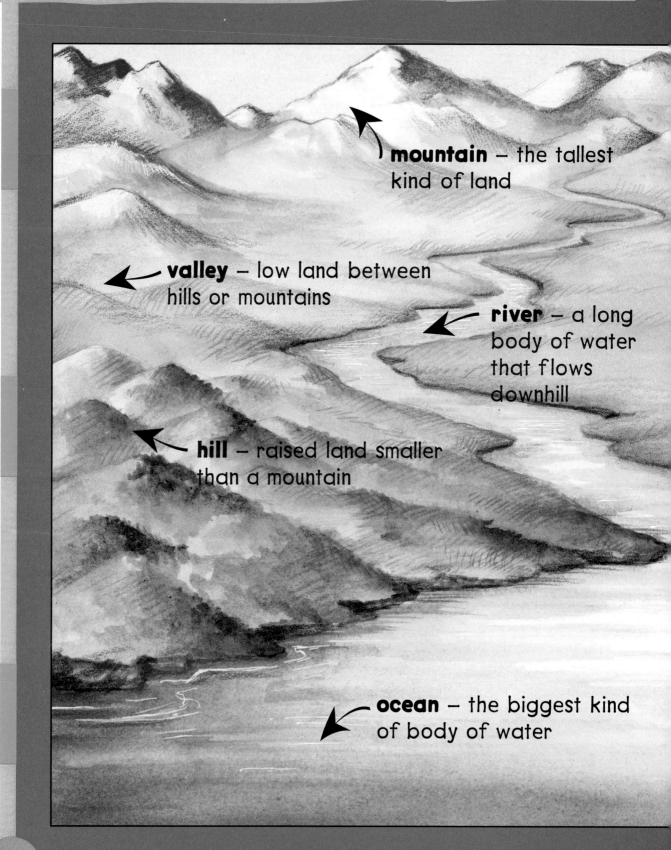

mountain – the tallest kind of land

valley – low land between hills or mountains

river – a long body of water that flows downhill

hill – raised land smaller than a mountain

ocean – the biggest kind of body of water

plain – flat land

lake – water that has land all around it

PICTURE GLOSSARY

ANCESTORS family members who lived before you were born. *Most* ancestors *of African Americans came from Africa.*

BAR GRAPH a chart that uses bars to show "how many." *This* bar graph *shows how many books we read.*

CALENDAR a chart that shows the months, weeks, and days of the year. *I used a* calendar *to find out what today's date is.*

CHART a way to show information simply. *This* chart *shows what pets we have.*

COMMUNITY people who live in the same area. *My* community *is made up of many different people.*

CONTINENT a large area of land on Earth. *North America is a* continent.

COUNTRY a land in which the people share a group of laws. *The United States is our* country.

DIRECTION North, south, east, and west are directions. *What direction is Mexico from the United States?*

EARTH the planet we live on. *The United States is on planet* Earth.

ENSLAVED owned and made to work without pay. *Millions of Africans were once* enslaved *in the United States.*

FAMILY the people you live with. *My mother, my father, my brother, my sister, and I are a* family.

GLOBE a model of planet Earth. *Can you find the United States on the* globe?

GOODS things that people buy and sell. *The store sells goods like fruits and vegetables.*

HISTORY a story about real events that happened long ago. *I am learning about the history of Detroit.*

Fort Detroit

MAIN IDEA the most important idea of a story. *The main idea of this story is that you should help other people.*

MAP a drawing of a place. *This map shows the United States.*

United States

MAP KEY a chart that helps people read a map. *The map shows a red box. The map key tells you it is a school.*

Map Key
House School Park Street

MONTH a part of a year. *We have a holiday in the month of January.*

Martin Luther King, Jr.'s Birthday

NATURAL RESOURCES things people use that come from nature. *Water and soil are natural resources.*

NEEDS things that people must have to live. *Food, clothing, and shelter are* needs.

NEIGHBORHOOD an area where people work, live, and play. *My* neighborhood *has two parks.*

PICTURE GRAPH a way to show "how many," using pictures. *This* picture graph *shows how many animals there are.*

PREDICTION a guess about something that might happen. *My* prediction *is that it will rain.*

RECYCLE to collect something and reuse it. *We* recycle *paper, plastic, glass, and metal.*

RELATIVES people who are in your family. *I went to visit my* relatives.

RULE something that tells people how to behave. *The* rule *for crossing the street is to wait for the "WALK" sign.*

SEASON a part of the year. *Winter is a cold* season *in many parts of the world.*

SERVICE something that people do to help others. *The firefighters do a* service *by putting out fires.*

SHELTER any place where people or animals live. *An apartment building is one form of* shelter.

STATE a large area that is part of a country. *Michigan is a* state *in the United States.*

SYMBOL something that stands for something else. *This flag is a* symbol *of the United States.*

TIME LINE a chart that shows when things happened. *This* time line *shows how I grew.*

TRANSPORTATION a way of moving people and things. *A bus offers one kind of* transportation.

VOLUNTEER a person who decides to be a helper. *The* volunteer *passes out lunch.*

VOTE a way to decide or choose something. *We had a* vote *for class helper.*

WANTS things people like, but do not need. *I do not need a bicycle, but it is one of my* wants.

WEATHER what the air outside is like. *The* weather *today is hot.*

INDEX

CREDITS

Art Credits
Unit 4: 82, 83: Roberta Collier Morales; 85, 93, 101: Dennis Dittrich; 86, 87: Rodica Prato; 93: Jerry McDaniel; 95, 96, 97: Anne Stanley; 98, 99: Teresa Anderko; Unit 5: 116, 117, 131: Rodica Prato; Unit 6: 136, 137, 151: Frank Ferri; 148, 149: Susan Blubaugh

Photo Credits
Front Cover: (top background) Gordon Alexander, (bottom background) Stephen Ogilvy, (top inset) Bill Lyons/Photo Researchers, Inc., (center inset) Darrell Lane, (bottom inset) Harvey Lloyd/The Stock Market, (right and left foreground) Stephen Ogilvy, (back cover) Gordon Alexander

Title Page: Stephen Ogilvy; iii: (top) Lawrence Migdale/Photo Reseachers, Inc., (bottom left, center, & right) Stephen Ogilvy; iv: (top left) K. Zimbardo/Liaison International, (top right) Bill Lyons/Liaison International, (left center) Prit Vesilind/NGS Image Collection, (right center) George Gerster/Photo Researchers, Inc., (bottom left) Betty Press/Woodfin Camp & Associates, (bottom right) Tom Bean; v: (top) William L. Hill, Jr./Stock Boston, (left center) Bob Daemmrich/Stock Boston, (right center) Corbis/Bettmann, (bottom left) Don Mason/The Stock Market, (model T) Corbis Images, (computer) Stephen Ogilvy; 76: (inset) Don Mason/The Stock Market; 76–77: (background) Gordon Alexander; 77: (top) Lawrence Migdale/Photo Reseachers, Inc., (bottom) Peter Fisher/The Stock Market; 78: (inset) Stephen Ogilvy; 78–79: (background) Bill Horsman/Stock Boston; 79: (top, bottom) Stephen Ogilvy; 80: Stephen Ogilvy; 81: Corbis/Kelley-Mooney Photography; 84, 85: Stephen Ogilvy; 88: (top) Chris Jones/The Stock Market, (bottom) Laima Druskis/Stock Boston; 89: Gordon Alexander; 90: (top) Stephen Ogilvy, (bottom) George E. Jones/Photo Researchers, Inc.; 91: Stephen Ogilvy; 94: (top) Jim Foster/The Stock Market, (bottom) Larry Fleming/AG Stock USA; 95: Vince Streano/The Stock Market; 96: (top) Larry Lefever/Grant Heilman Photography, (bottom) Charles West/The Stock Market; 97: Stephen Ogilvy; 100: T & D McCarthy/The Stock Market; 102: (top inset) Bill Lyons/Photo Researchers, Inc., (bottom inset) Betty Press/Woodfin Camp & Associates; 102–103 (background) Copyright 1999, PhotoDisc, Inc.; 103: (top inset) Corbis/Nik Wheeler, (bottom inset) Catherine Karnow/Woodfin Camp & Associates; 104: (inset): Corbis/Paul Almasy; 104–105: (background) Corbis/Werner Forman; 105: (top) Betty Press/Woodfin Camp & Associates, (bottom) George Gerster/Photo Researchers, Inc.; 106: (top) Corbis/Nik Wheeler, (bottom) Wendy V. Watriss/Woodfin Camp & Associates; 107: (top & bottom) David Sutherland; 108: (top inset) Tony Arruza/Bruce Coleman, Inc., (bottom inset) Tom Bean/The Stock Market; 108–109: (background) Tom Bean/The Stock Market; 109: (inset) Rita Nanni/Photo Researchers, Inc.; 110: M. Mastrorillo/The Stock Market; 111: (top) Tom Bean, (bottom) Stephen Ogilvy; 112: (inset) Harvey Lloyd/The Stock Market; 112–113: (background) Yves Marcoux/Tony Stone Images; 113: (inset) Cosmo Condina/Tony Stone Images; 114: (top) Prit Vesilind/NGS Image Collection, (bottom) David Travers/The Stock Market; 115: Ariel Skelley/The Stock Market; 118: (inset) Mike Yamashita/Woodfin Camp & Associates; 118–119: (background) Catherine Karnow/Woodfin Camp & Associates; 119: (top inset) Tibor Bognar/The Stock Market, (bottom inset) John Elk III/Bruce Coleman, Inc.; 120: (top) David Harvey/NGS Image Collection, (bottom) K. Zimbardo/Liaison International; 121: Harvey Lloyd/The Stock Market; 122: (top inset) Bill Lyons/Liaison International, (bottom inset) J. Polleross/The Stock Market; 122–123: (background) David Peterson/Tony Stone Images; 123: (inset) Margaret Kols/The Stock Market; 124: Corbis/Michelle Garrett; 125: Joanna Pinneo/NGS Image Collection; 126: (top left) Harvey Lloyd/The Stock Market, (top right) M & E Bernheim/Woodfin Camp & Asssociates, (bottom) John Chard/Tony Stone Images; 127: (top) Corbis/Charles O'Rear, (center) Corbis/Paul Almasy, (bottom) Gianni Tortoli/Photo Researchers, Inc.; 128: (top left & top right) Darrell Lane, (bottom left) Renee Lynn/Photo Researchers, Inc., (bottom right) Darrell Lane; 129: (top & bottom) Betty Press/Woodfin Camp & Associates; 130: Angelo Cavcalli/The Image Bank; 132: (background) Copyright 1999, Photodisc, Inc., (inset) Michael A. Keller/The Stock Market; 132–133: (background) Copyright 1999, Photodisc, Inc.; 133: (top inset) FPG International, (bottom inset) Michael Newman/PhotoEdit; 134: (top) Don Mason: The Stock Market, (bottom) Paul Barton/The Stock Market; 135: (computer) Stephen Ogilvy, (Model T) Corbis Images; 138: (left) Stephen Ogilvy, (top right) Bob Daemmrich/Stock Boston, (bottom right) Rhoda Sidney/Stock Boston; 139: (top) Jose L. Pelaez/The Stock Market, (bottom) Gabe Palmer/The Stock Market; 140: (top) David Young-Wolff/PhotoEdit, (bottom) William L. Hill, Jr./Stock Boston; 141: (top) José Luis Palaez/The Stock Market, (bottom) C/B Productions/The Stock Market; 142: FPG International; 143: Ira Montgomery/The Image Bank; 144: H. Armstrong Roberts/The Stock Market; 145: Spencer Grant/PhotoEdit; 146: Corbis/Bettmann; 147: Benelux/Photo Researchers, Inc.; 150: Elaine Sulle/The Image Bank